Rabbit Magic

Rabbit Magic

by Carol Beach York
illustrated by Irene Trivas

A
LITTLE APPLE
PAPERBACK

SCHOLASTIC INC.
New York Toronto London Auckland Sydney

ISBN 0-590-43894-8

Copyright © 1991 by Carol Beach York.
Illustrations copyright © 1991 by Scholastic Inc.
All rights reserved. Published by Scholastic Inc.

APPLE PAPERBACKS is a registered trademark of Scholastic Inc.

12 11 10 9 8 7 6 5 4 3 2 1   1 2 3 4 5 6/9

Printed in the U.S.A.   40
First Scholastic printing, March 1991

For Roger and Donna
and the rabbits they love

CONTENTS

Rabbit Magic

The Muffin Delivery

It was a golden Saturday afternoon in Butterfield Square. The sky was bright with sunshine as the last of the autumn leaves fluttered from the trees. All the fine old brick houses looked cheerful, with their stone steps and iron gates and sparkling windows. At Number 18, The Good Day Orphanage for Girls, the handyman raked the leaves into a pile by the backyard fence.

In the kitchen, Cook was baking blueberry muffins. Rack upon rack, muffin tins filled up the big oven.

Miss Plum and Miss Lavender, the two ladies who took care of the twenty-eight girls who lived at The Good Day, sat in the parlor. Miss Plum was a thin, plainly dressed woman with her hair in a twist on top of her head. Miss Lavender wore ruffles and frills and combed her hair in fluffy curls. She was usually very joyful and light-hearted, but not today. She wished to speak to Miss Plum about something very important, a sort of secret. But she was afraid Miss Plum wouldn't understand. Miss Plum might even laugh.

Miss Lavender pretended to be interested in her mending — Good Day girls were always losing buttons and outgrowing hems — but she couldn't pay attention. She tried to think of just the right way to tell Miss Plum her secret.

I've just thought of something that would be fun, was one way she might begin. But that wouldn't be exactly right because she had not "just thought" of it. She thought of it many years ago when she was no bigger than The Good Day girls.

Perhaps she could say, *Have you ever had something you always wanted to do and never did?*

Or she might ask, oh so very casually, *Have you seen the paper today? . . .* but no, that wouldn't do at all. Of course, Miss Plum had seen the paper. It was at this moment right in front of her on her desk.

Miss Plum had sat down at her desk to go over grocery bills, but the crossword puzzle in the morning newspaper caught her eye. She thought she would try just a few words before she started on the household bills. She had already found a six-letter word for a small lake that is not a lake — *lagoon;* a seven-letter word for a boat that tows other boats — *tugboat;* a ten-letter word for a fake diamond — *rhinestone.* Now she needed a three-letter word for an Australian bird that could not fly.

In the kitchen, the muffins were just coming out of the oven, hot and sweet, bursting with blueberries. They were beautiful to see, as things Cook made always were. Cook had a round, jolly face, and she loved her kitchen — the heat of the oven, the smell of good things baking, soups simmering, and spices in the air.

Now she thought she would like to send

some warm muffins to the ladies in the parlor — if she could find someone to take them.

Usually it wasn't hard to find someone, not with twenty-eight girls living right there at The Good Day. Sure enough, Cook had no sooner thought of sending muffins to the parlor than Tatty and Phoebe ran in from the backyard. They had been running through the leaves one last time before the handyman got them all raked up.

Phoebe had led the race through the leaves, scuffling her feet and beating her arms against her sides as if she were riding a horse. As soon as she came through the kitchen door, she held her hands to her heart and closed her eyes. "Oh, what a wonderful smell — oh, what a heavenly smell — oh, I have *never* smelled anything so delicious. . . ."

"Yes," said Cook, to quiet Phoebe, "you may have a muffin. Then you may take some to the ladies."

Cook gave Tatty a muffin, too.

Tatty was seven years old. She didn't always get her dress buttons into the right buttonholes, and her hair ribbons fell off and got lost. Today she had fallen down in the leaves, and bits of dried leaves and stems stuck to her sweater. She didn't look neat enough to deliver muffins to the parlor, but Cook said she could go along.

While Tatty and Phoebe bit into their muffins, Cook fixed a nice plate for Miss Lavender and Miss Plum. She put napkins on top for the ladies to use when they ate. Tatty and Phoebe were licking muffin crumbs from their fingers when a girl named Kate came bounding in. (She always bounded wherever she went.) She got a muffin, too, and went off to share it with the brown sparrows and blue jays that lived in the Butterfield Square park.

From the parlor window Miss Plum saw Kate darting across to the park, sprinkling muffin crumbs for the birds. . . . "Miss Lavender," she said, turning toward the sofa, "what is a three-letter word for an Australian bird that cannot fly?"

"Not much of a bird, if you ask me," Miss Lavender said absently. Her mind was, of course, on her secret. She had just opened her mouth to tell Miss Plum at last, when Tatty and Phoebe came in with the plate of muffins.

"For you, madams," Phoebe said as she grandly swept off the napkins and waved the plate of muffins for the ladies to see.

So Miss Lavender couldn't tell her secret just then after all.

Miss Lavender's Secret

The parlor was so noisy now — just when Miss Lavender wanted to talk *privately*.

Tatty was plinking on the piano with two fingers that were not very clean. Little Ann — the smallest of all The Good Day girls, only five years old — came in with a watering can to ask if she could water the plants on the windowsill.

Miss Plum and Little Ann hovered over the plants, Tatty plinked the piano, and Phoebe whirled around to see if she could make herself dizzy. Miss Lavender pricked a finger as she tried to sew. "You are like a cyclone, Phoebe!" she said.

Phoebe flew to the dictionary on the table by the window and read:

A cyclone is a storm of winds spinning

around a center of low atmospheric pressure.

I am a storm of winds, she thought with a thrill.

Cook sent tea to go with the muffins, and three girls came bearing the tray and the teapot and the cups and saucers and sugar bowl and spoons. Elsie May, the oldest girl and very bossy, led this parade. Little Ann dropped her watering can onto the windowsill, and Elsie May said, "Look what you've done!" as water spurted onto the carpet. Tatty plinked louder on the piano, and Phoebe began to spin again like a storm of winds.

The girls who had brought the tea things arranged them on a table by the sofa. There was clinking and clanking as the spoons were put here and there; no girl was sure whether spoons should go into the cups or on the saucers — or perhaps somewhere else entirely. Only the teapot, squarely in the middle of the table, was left alone. Tatty began to sing along with her piano playing. Kate arrived back from the park and began to whirl around with Phoebe until they both fell in a heap.

Ah, thought Miss Lavender, threading a needle, *it can't be helped. When you live with twenty-eight children, there isn't always peace and quiet.*

But by and by it got quiet. All the girls ran back outside — except Elsie May, who thought she was too grown-up to play. She went to do something more important, to admire herself in a mirror perhaps, or comb out her long yellow braids, or write in her diary.

The ladies were alone again. Miss Plum took her cup of tea to her desk, frowning, for the problem of the Australian bird was not solved.

The muffins had cooled some, but the tea was still hot. Miss Lavender took a sip. Now was her chance. She looked over her teacup at Miss Plum and began boldly.

"Have you ever thought it would be fun to learn some magic?"

Miss Plum had not been expecting this question. "Magic?" She turned away from her crossword puzzle looking surprised. "What kind of magic?"

"Oh, you know." Miss Lavender shrugged her shoulders lightly and tried to look wise. "Just magic. Haven't you ever wanted to be able to do some magic?"

Miss Plum thought for a moment. She was very kind and wise. She always knew what was best to do when there was a crisis. She was what you might call the "backbone" of The Good Day. But she never had any desire to be a magician. "No," she said slowly, "I've never wanted to be able to do magic."

"I have," Miss Lavender confessed in a rush. "I've always longed to, ever since I was a small child."

"Is that so?" Miss Plum listened politely. She was not sure where all this was leading.

"Yes, yes, I have," Miss Lavender said. Then she didn't know what to say next.

"You mean magic tricks, like pulling pennies from behind people's ears, and rabbits from hats, that sort of thing?"

"Yes, *exactly*." Miss Lavender looked enormously relieved. "Now that you mention it, the rabbit-in-the-hat trick would be just the thing for a beginning. Actually, I did see something in the newspaper just this morning — an advertisement. . . ." She put aside the sewing basket and came to the desk where Miss Plum had spread open the newspaper to work the crossword puzzle. "It's near the back — page twelve — ah, here we are."

Miss Plum watched in some bewilderment as Miss Lavender turned the pages of the paper. The crossword puzzle disappeared from view. Other pages went by, and then at last Miss Lavender paused at page twelve and pointed triumphantly to a rather small advertisement.

Learn Amazing Feats of Magic

The Great Rudolpho, famous on all continents, performer for crowned heads of Europe, can teach you incredible feats of magic. He is willing to share the miracle secrets of the art of legerdemain, beginning with the most time-honored of all magicians' skills: pulling a rabbit from a hat. Amaze and mystify your friends. Delight children. The fee is small, the rewards are great.

For further information, write to:

The Great Rudolpho c/o this newspaper.

"I thought I might write," Miss Lavender said, when Miss Plum had read the advertisement. "You know, for the further information."

She was so excited about the idea, she hoped Miss Plum wouldn't say it was all silly nonsense.

What Miss Plum did say was wonderful. "Well, dear Miss Lavender, if this is something you have wanted for so long, I see no harm in it. If it is a true heart's desire, write, by all means."

"I'm so glad you feel that way." Miss Lavender breathed a sigh of relief. "I'll write at once. I'll write to The Great Rudolpho this very minute."

And she did.

The Great Rudolpho

The Great Rudolpho responded very quickly to Miss Lavender's letter. He called her on the telephone and made an appointment to come see her and discuss her magic lessons.

When the afternoon for this appointment arrived, Miss Lavender couldn't sit still. She peered out the windows to see if The Great Rudolpho was coming. She thought all the clocks had stopped, the minutes went by so slowly. She wanted her magic lessons to *begin*.

"I think I'll go out into the yard for a breath of fresh air," she said at last (the better to watch for The Great Rudolpho).

"A good idea," Miss Plum said. She couldn't concentrate on anything with Miss Lavender fidgeting.

16

It was just past three o'clock, and the girls were returning from school.

Kate was doing cartwheels on grassy spots along the way, and Phoebe hopped on one leg. She wanted to see if she could hop all the way home. She had to lean on things and rest a lot, and she was glad to collapse at last against the gate to The Good Day's front yard.

There was Miss Lavender getting her breath of fresh air. She moved to the gate at once, too excited to keep her news to herself. "Guess what I'm doing," Miss Lavender said. Before Phoebe or Kate could answer, she rushed on: "I'm waiting for someone who is going to teach me magic."

"*Magic!*"

Kate and Phoebe were as excited as Miss Lavender. "Who's going to teach you?" "Can we watch?" They were both talking at once.

"The Great Rudolpho is going to teach me," Miss Lavender said. "No, I don't think you will be able to watch. I think magic lessons are secret. But you can meet The Great Rudolpho if you like. Oh, I believe I see him coming at last."

Up the street came a large man with flowing dark hair, alertly reading house numbers. He wore a blue velvet coat with a flower in his buttonhole, and he whipped the air with a silver-handled cane as he walked.

It had to be The Great Rudolpho. Magic seemed to hum around him. He had an aura of stage lights and applause — bouquets of flowers might unfold from his coat sleeves at any moment, a lady might be sawed in half, a piece of paper cut into a thousand pieces and put back whole again in the wink of an eye. When he came to the gate, he swept off his hat. The girls expected a rabbit to come from it. No rabbit was in his hat, but it was indeed the man himself — The Great Rudolpho.

"My dear lady," he said, greeting Miss Lavender as if she were a queen.

Then they went indoors, leaving Kate

and Phoebe staring after them.

As the other girls came back from school, Phoebe and Kate told them the news of Miss Lavender's magic lessons. They all talked about what a wonderful thing it was.

Inside, Miss Lavender led The Great Rudolpho to the parlor and introduced him to Miss Plum.

"My pleasure, Madam," The Great Rudolpho said as he kissed her hand.

After saying hello to the gentleman, Miss Plum left the parlor so Miss Lavender could have her magic lesson.

To Miss Lavender's disappointment she discovered that the lessons could not begin at once.

"No, no," The Great Rudolpho said. "First the equipment, then the lessons."

He placed his hat and cane on a chair by the parlor window. He removed his coat, flower and all. Underneath the blue coat The Great Rudolpho wore a black suit, which he had bought at some thinner time in his life, and a magnificent shirt with pink stripes. When he drew off his gloves, his fingers sparkled with rings.

"What kind of equipment?" Miss Lavender asked.

"You wish to pull the rabbit from the hat?"

"Yes, I do."

"To practice you must have the rabbits. This is so?"

"Well . . . I only want to pull out one rabbit," Miss Lavender explained.

The Great Rudolpho held up a hand. "Is true. But to learn to pull even one rabbit from the hat, you must practice, practice, practice. For this you must have many rabbits."

Miss Lavender was surprised. Before she could say anything, The Great Rudolpho continued: "And hutches for the rabbits, food for the rabbits. All this I will supply. The cost is small."

The bejeweled hand brushed away any worries about cost. "And of course, the hat," he said. "One cannot pull the rabbit from the hat without the hat. Is true?"

"Yes, that's certainly true," Miss Lavender agreed. She hesitated and then said, "I've just always thought real magic didn't need real things, that's what made it truly magic."

The Great Rudolpho looked shocked. "Is impossible," he said, casting his great dark eyes upon Miss Lavender. "You must have the rabbits or how will you do this?" He seemed very disturbed.

"I'm sorry," Miss Lavender said. "I didn't mean to upset you."

"Is all right," The Great Rudolpho said. But he sighed a deep sigh and shook his heavy, dark-flowing hair in a discouraged way.

"I'll buy the rabbits and the hutches," Miss Lavender said quickly. "And the food, of course — that, too."

The Great Rudolpho looked a little less distressed. "And the hat," he reminded her.

"Yes, and the hat." Miss Lavender was warming to the idea. She would soon have her very own magician's hat.

"I send the rabbits in the morning," The Great Rudolpho promised. "In the afternoon we have the lesson."

The Rabbitry

The next morning, just as The Great Rudolpho had promised, the rabbits, the rabbit hutches, and the rabbit food arrived at Number 18 Butterfield Square.

All these things came in a green delivery van with a white sign lettered on the side: QUICK DELIVERY SERVICE. A man in blue overalls and jacket carried twelve hutches into the backyard, each with a plump, furry rabbit inside. There were also several burlap bags full of lettuce, carrots, and cabbage leaves for the rabbits to eat. Last but not least, the delivery man gave Miss Lavender a tall, shiny black silk hat — a true magician's hat.

With all this excitement, no one could stay inside. Even Cook came out to the yard to see it all.

The morning was clear and bright. Most of the trees were bare of leaves, and the chill of winter-to-come was in the air. It was a day when a fire in the fireplace was cheerful, and the time of year when apples were most crisp and juicy.

"These are my practice rabbits," Miss Lavender explained to the girls. "And this is my magician's hat."

All the girls loved the beautiful black hat. When Tatty tried it on, it slid straight down over her head and hid her whole face. It was not her size.

But it was the rabbits the girls loved the most.

There were tan rabbits and brown rabbits, gray rabbits with black eyes, white rabbits with red eyes and tinges of pink in their long rabbit ears. The girls stood around the hutches, touching the wire sides carefully, saying, "Hello, rabbit. Hello, rabbit."

The rabbits were silent, with quivering noses. They were bigger than anyone expected them to be — and very beautiful and mysterious.

"Will they be cold out here?" Tatty asked. Her hair needed combing; her stockings needed a good tug up. She turned to Miss Lavender with a worried expression. She didn't want the rabbits to be cold.

"Cold won't bother them," Cook said. "Rabbits can keep warm easily enough. It's the hot weather, summer weather, that bothers them more."

"What do they eat?" redheaded Mary wanted to know. The burlap bags were still tightly shut, and she didn't know what was inside.

"They eat lettuce and carrots," Cook said. "Sometimes alfalfa hay. They like dry oatmeal and bread, too."

"How do you know all that?" Miss Lavender was impressed.

"My brother and I had rabbits when we were children," Cook said. "My brother has rabbits still. He raises them on his farm."

"Can you give them a bath?" Tatty asked.

"No need to," Cook said. "Rabbits wash themselves, just like cats do."

"How old do they live to be?" Phoebe asked, wiggling a finger through the wires of the cage of a splendid white rabbit with long silky hair and ruby-red eyes.

Cook had to think a minute about that. "About eight or ten years, as I recall. They're born blind, like kittens. I recall that, too."

The girls stared at the rabbits, thinking about all this.

"And they're born bare," Cook added. "The hair comes later."

Miss Lavender was relieved. "Thank goodness you know so much about rabbits."

Cook smiled modestly. It was time for her to get back to her kitchen. "Well," she said as she started for the back door, "this is a fine rabbitry, a fine rabbitry."

"What's a rabbitry?" Mary asked, tagging after Cook.

"It's a rabbit farm," said Cook, and she disappeared into her kitchen.

"When the man comes, can we watch your magic lesson?" Tatty asked.

Again Miss Lavender said the lesson was private. "However, you may meet The Great Rudolpho when he comes," she offered.

All the girls wanted to meet him. Phoebe and Kate wanted to see him again, strutting along with his cane, and his high hat, and the flower in his buttonhole.

"He's coming at two," Miss Lavender said. At two o'clock all the girls gathered by the front gate to watch for The Great Rudolpho. Miss Lavender and Miss Plum looked out from the parlor window.

Time went by.

More time went by.

And then *more* time went by.

The hands of the mantel clock pointed to ten minutes past two, then to twenty minutes past two.

Girls came in from the yard to say that The Great Rudolpho had not yet come.

"I'm sure he'll be along any minute," Miss Lavender said.

Miss Plum held her ear to the mantel clock to hear if it was ticking.

Some of the girls stayed by the front gate, but they grew tired of waiting and went to the backyard to look at the rabbits again. It was exciting to have a rabbitry right in their own yard, and exciting that Miss Lavender was going to learn magic.

But where was The Great Rudolpho?

A Sad Day

Twenty-seven past two . . . two-thirty . . . a quarter to three.

Time hurried on, but The Great Rudolpho did not come.

At three o'clock Miss Plum said, "I fear you have been tricked, Miss Lavender."

"Oh, dear." Miss Lavender looked upset.

"Yes, I definitely think you have been tricked," Miss Plum said. "It seems The Great Rudolpho was only trying to rid himself of twelve rabbits. I fancy he is going out of the rabbit-in-the-hat business and wished to make a profit, however underhanded. The act of a charlatan."

Miss Lavender was very disappointed. "I did so very much want to learn some magic," she said. "The Great Rudolpho seemed just the one to teach me."

Miss Plum shook her head. "We are both sadder and wiser. I hope you didn't pay much. I fear your money is gone forever."

"Oh . . . not very much . . ." Miss Lavender answered vaguely. She didn't really want to tell how much she had paid. It *had* seemed to her rather a lot for twelve rabbits, even with hutches and food, even with a tall black hat.

It was a sad day at Number 18 Butterfield Square. All efforts to trace The Great Rudolpho through the newspaper where he had placed the advertisement came to nothing. He had vanished completely, taking Miss Lavender's good money and leaving the rabbits behind.

Miss Lavender only wanted to learn some magic. She didn't want a backyard full of rabbits. Fortunately, Cook said her brother, who raised rabbits, would be happy to have them. The twelve hutches were loaded into a delivery van again and sent off to the country, where Miss Lavender was sure the rabbits would have a good home.

Miss Lavender kept the black magician's hat because it was too beautiful to part with. Maybe someday it would come in useful.

A few days after the van had gone rumbling off into the countryside with the rabbits, Miss Lavender and Miss Plum were sitting in the parlor having tea. The twenty-eight girls were at school, and it was not (thank heaven) Mr. Not So Much's day.

Mr. Not So Much was on the Board of Directors of The Good Day. His duty was to come once a month and look over the expenses, the money matters. Money was very important to Mr. Not So Much. He did not approve of spending it. When he came to The Good Day, he always found too much money being spent, and he said so. "Not so much money, ladies! Not so much money!" As he spoke, he rapped on tabletops and paced around the parlor. He glowered and glared. Nobody liked his visits.

However, he was not there this peaceful afternoon.

Outside, the last few brown leaves rustled along the ground when the wind blew. The sky was rather dark, and Miss Plum lit the lamps in the parlor. Now she poured the tea. Her kindly eyes were filled with sympathy for Miss Lavender. "Try not to feel too bad about all this," she said gently.

"It was a true heart's desire," Miss Lavender reminded her. For a true heart's desire, one had a right to feel bad. "Anyway, I haven't given up," she added. "I'm sure there is a way I can do *something* magical. No, I'll not give up yet."

A Magic Potion

Phoebe and Kate made up some magic words, to cheer up Miss Lavender.

But the magic words didn't change a tree into a burning candle, a shoe into an elephant, or a spoon into a butterfly, as they were supposed to do.

"We can pretend," Phoebe said.

Miss Lavender wanted more than "pretend."

Cook said perhaps Miss Lavender should try card tricks. She even had a book Miss Lavender could use.

"That's not *magic,*" Miss Lavender said, but Cook brought the book to show her. Right on the cover it said:

101 CARD TRICKS
*Amaze your friends with
the magic of card tricks.*

"Well, it's cheaper than buying a lot of rabbits," Miss Plum reminded Miss Lavender. Cook was lending the book free.

So Miss Lavender read the book. And one afternoon when she felt she was ready to amaze her friends, she gathered together three Good Day girls — Tatty, Mary, and Little Ann.

"Choose a card, Tatty," she said, "any card." Miss Lavender fanned out a deck of playing cards and kept her eyes closed while Tatty chose one. "Now show your card to everyone," Miss Lavender directed.

"Everyone" was only Mary and Little Ann. Little Ann didn't know much about cards, so Mary had to whisper in her ear, "It's the King of Hearts."

"Now put the card back into the deck," Miss Lavender told Tatty. Her eyes were still closed so she wouldn't see Tatty's card.

Tatty put the card back into the deck, and Miss Lavender held the cards in her hand. She shuffled them. Once. Twice. Then she drew out a card. "Here is your

card," she said triumphantly.

But it wasn't Tatty's card. It was the Three of Spades.

Little Ann was confused.

"That's not it," Mary said politely.

"Are you sure?" Miss Lavender looked at the card closely. If she was to succeed at card tricks, this should be Tatty's card. "What was your card, Tatty?" she asked.

"The King of Hearts."

Miss Lavender slumped in her chair. "Ah," she said, "I have failed again."

Little Ann patted Miss Lavender's hand tenderly. Miss Lavender smiled and looked into Little Ann's blue eyes. "What shall I do now, Little Ann?" she asked with a sigh. "Maybe I should try to make a magic potion of some sort. . . . Yes, perhaps I'll do that. Well, I'll have to think about it."

There were no more card tricks, so Little Ann followed Tatty and Mary to the park to play. The park was brown and bare now. The fountain was only cold white stone. They began a game of tag, and then they met Phoebe, throwing a ball against a tree. They told her about Miss Lavender's card trick.

"She was very sad when it didn't work," Mary said. "She's going to make a magic potion next."

Phoebe's face lit up. "Why don't we make a magic potion, too! I bet Cook would let us."

They raced back to The Good Day and burst into Cook's kitchen out of breath.

"Here now," said Cook. "What's all this?" When she heard they were going to make a magic potion, she was very interested. "What will you put into it?" she asked. Her dinner preparations were well underway — with cherry pie for dessert — and she had time to chat.

"We can start with water," said Mary, thinking hard.

"I've got that," said Cook.

"And some lemons," Tatty said, catching sight of a lemon on the kitchen table.

"And sugar," said Little Ann.

"This is *not* lemonade," Phoebe reminded everybody. "This is a magic potion."

In the end, they mixed up water and lemon juice, cinnamon, parsley flakes, and sweet basil leaves from Cook's spice cabinet. Then they were ready.

"I'll go first," Phoebe said boldly. This was only right, as making the potion was her idea.

Phoebe drank a few drops.

Little Ann drank a few drops.

Mary drank a few drops.

Tatty drank a few drops.

Cook decided she was not thirsty after all. "Anyway," she said, "it's time to cook my carrots."

"Yuck!" Phoebe said. She didn't like vegetables.

Outside, the girls sat down on the back steps and waited for the magic potion to take effect.

"What will happen?" Tatty asked Phoebe.

"What does the magic potion do?"

Phoebe thought a moment. "It will make us fly," she decided.

Then, as the day grew dark and the autumn winds blew across the park, Tatty and Mary and Phoebe and Little Ann spread their arms like wings and flew about The Good Day yard. They swooped and turned and wheeled and zoomed into the wonderful cold air.

"What are you *doing*?" Elsie May said with her nose stuck up as usual. She was twelve, the oldest of all The Good Day girls. She had two yellow braids, tied with ribbon. When she combed them out, her hair was all ripples from being braided, and no one was allowed to touch it.

"We're flying!" Phoebe shouted. She swung on the front gate, flapping her arms. "We made a magic potion and we're flying."

"We're flying!" said Little Ann as she tumbled down under a bush.

"We're flying — we're flying!" Tatty and Mary flapped and giggled and ran in every direction at once.

Elsie May put her nose up a notch higher and marched through the front door. She marched right down the hall and into the parlor. Miss Plum and Miss Lavender were by the fire. Now that the days were chilly, they liked a nice cheery fire burning in the fireplace.

If Mr. Not So Much had been there, he would not have liked the fire at all. Burning fires cost money. It was like burning money, he always said. Good thing he was not there!

"Tatty and Phoebe and Mary and Little Ann are running all over the yard," Elsie May complained. "They say they're flying. They say they made a magic potion and they're flying."

Miss Plum lifted her head from the book she was reading. "Magic, magic," she murmured, shaking her head. "Is that all anyone thinks of these days?"

Miss Lavender peeped out the window to see the girls. Ah, it looked like so much fun . . . flying in the dusky yard as night-time came.

Mr. Not So Much

After she had failed at card tricks, Miss Lavender gave her deck of cards to the girls.

They played Go Fish and built card houses and colored the cards that were only plain black and white. The Queen of Clubs got lost first, and then the Seven of Diamonds. By and by, all the cards were worn, raggedy, sticky, or lost.

Miss Lavender returned *101 Card Tricks* to Cook. "Thanks just the same," she said, "but I have no knack for card tricks."

She was discouraged. Cook could see that. "I had a cousin once who could tell the meaning of dreams," Cook told Miss Lavender. "Maybe you could learn to do that."

"Do you think so?"

"I expect it only takes practice," Cook said.

Miss Lavender agreed to try. She had nothing to lose.

"Begin tonight," Cook urged. "Forget card tricks. Dreams are more important."

That night Miss Lavender went to bed at exactly ten o'clock, which was her habit. She fell sound asleep at once and dreamed she was riding in a bus that turned into a boat. When she saw she was in a boat, she felt anxious because she didn't know if the Captain would accept a bus ticket. A bus ticket was all she had in her pocketbook.

Tickets, tickets please, the Captain called out, coming closer and closer.

Then he disappeared in a puff of smoke before he reached Miss Lavender.

When Miss Lavender woke in the morning, she remembered the dream for a few moments. It began to slide away from her long before she had decided what it was all about. Before she was even out of bed, the dream had entirely vanished from her mind, never to return, never to be properly understood.

Outside, the day was gloomy. *Exactly the way I feel,* Miss Lavender thought. It seemed a long time since The Great Rudolpho had come, glittering with rings, and Miss Lavender's hopes had been high.

And the day did not improve. Mr. Not So Much was due for his monthly visit, and at three o'clock he arrived stern and frowning at The Good Day's front door. If he had his way, he would have renamed the whole place The Bad Day, for he could never find anything "good" about it. The girls were too noisy. The ladies spent too much money. Cook cooked too much food. Money flew up the fireplace chimney as firewood burned.

Mr. Not So Much always dressed in black, as if for a funeral. He was thin and fierce-looking even when he smiled, which he hardly ever did.

A girl named Nonnie answered his knock at the door. And then she ran away, which was the best thing to do when Mr. Not So Much was around. In the parlor he found Miss Plum at her desk. He settled himself in a chair and took off his gloves. He was just pulling out his gold pocket watch to see the time when Miss Lavender came into the parlor.

She didn't care much for Mr. Not So Much. He was too stingy and fussy for her. But on this particular afternoon she forgot everything else when she saw the fine gold watch he held. A fine gold watch on a fine gold chain.

A wonderful idea came to Miss Lavender, right at that moment in the parlor doorway. A *wonderful* idea.

Perhaps it was the answer to her problem!

The Gold Watch

"Ah, here's Miss Lavender." Miss Plum turned toward the doorway. She was glad not to have to put up with Mr. Not So Much all by herself.

Miss Lavender had eyes only for the gold watch Mr. Not So Much held in his hand.

"What a splendid watch!" she exclaimed, stepping into the parlor.

Mr. Not So Much could only agree. The watch was his most prized possession. It kept him aware of the time, and time was money. He consulted the watch often in the course of his daily activities. He had it out now because he couldn't trust the mantel clock. Sometimes it wasn't even running because no one at The Good Day had remembered to wind it.

"It's just what I need," Miss Lavender

continued. Cook came in with a tea tray, but Miss Lavender hardly noticed.

"With that watch, Mr. Not So Much, I can give a demonstration of hypnotism. Or at least I'd like to try."

Miss Plum looked surprised. "Do you know how to hypnotize people?" she asked. She was not sure she approved of hypnotism. How was it done, for one thing? Was it entirely safe? Was a person hypnotized forever after, or did it wear off in time?

"I saw a demonstration once," Miss Lavender said. "I was only a child, but I've never forgotten it."

Cook was listening, all ears.

"All I need is a gold watch on a chain, and here we have one."

Mr. Not So Much was silent. He did not want to lend his magnificent watch for a demonstration of hypnotism.

"Oh, please, let's try," Cook spoke up eagerly without warning. "I've always wanted to be hypnotized."

"You have?" Miss Plum was surprised again. "You never told me."

Cook blushed, embarrassed now that everyone was looking at her. "Yes, I always have wanted . . ." She looked at Mr. Not So Much hopefully, and it would have been quite rude of him to refuse to hand over his watch.

"Just for a few minutes," he warned. Then he sat scowling in a far-off chair.

Miss Lavender got Cook arranged comfortably on the sofa. Cook folded her hands. "Just keep your eyes on the watch," Miss Lavender crooned.

She swung the watch on the gold chain. It glittered in the firelight as it moved back and forth in front of Cook's face. "Just keep your eyes on the watch . . . keep your eyes on the watch . . . now you are getting drowsy . . . very drowsy . . . you are very sleepy now . . . very sleepy now . . . very sleepy — your eyes are closing."

Cook's eyes closed.

"Now you are drifting asleep . . . asleep . . . a lovely deep sleep," Miss Lavender continued softly.

Several girls peeked around the parlor doorway to see what was going on.

"Now I am going to count to ten," Miss Lavender said. "When I reach ten, you will waken . . . you will be refreshed from a lovely sleep . . . and you will be hungry . . . you will ask for a slice of bread."

Miss Plum sat forward in her chair rather anxiously. Her tea grew cold.

Miss Lavender paused a moment. Then she began to count. "One . . . two . . ."

Cook's eyes flew open.

"I'm not really asleep," she said apologetically. "I just had my eyes closed."

Miss Lavender was disapponted. "Not even a little drowsy?" she asked.

"I'm afraid not."

Over in his corner, Mr. Not So Much felt a little drowsy, but he gave himself a shake. He was grateful no one was watching. Such foolishness!

"I have failed at hypnotism, too," Miss Lavender had to admit. Reluctantly she gave Mr. Not So Much his watch. He examined it carefully to see that it was still in good condition.

"Yes, I have failed again." Miss Lavender sank down in a chair, feeling sad.

The girls peeking at the door came into the parlor — Tatty, Little Ann, and Phoebe. Little Ann stood by Miss Lavender's chair and patted her knee. Phoebe said right out, "You don't have to do magic, Miss Lavender. We like you just the way you are."

"You have been trying magic?" Mr. Not So Much had not heard this before. Nobody told him anything. "Best left alone, I'd say."

Cook was, of course, disappointed, too. "I've always wanted to be hypnotized," she said regretfully. As an afterthought she added, "And I've always wanted to go to a séance and talk to the spirit world."

"You have?" Once again Miss Plum was surprised. "You never told me."

Cook nodded her head. Tatty and Little Ann and Phoebe stared at her curiously. "The spirit world is" — Cook searched for just the right words to explain to them — "the spirit world is, well, it's people who have gone on."

Mr. Not So Much thought he had heard enough nonsense for one day. He got up stiffly and glanced around to see where he had put his hat.

"Who would you like to talk to in the spirit world?" Miss Lavender asked Cook. "We might try, you know. We could have our own séance. We could have it right here in the parlor. I could go into a trance."

Ah, maybe at this she would succeed. She felt a thrill of hope.

"Who would I like to contact in the spirit world? Well, now, let me think." Cook had not expected to have to choose someone from the spirit world to talk to that afternoon.

The girls waited while Cook thought. Little Ann leaned against Miss Lavender's knees. Tatty and Phoebe sat cross-legged on the floor by Miss Lavender's chair.

The parlor was silent.

Outside, the afternoon grew darker. It was time for Cook to be busy with dinner preparations. But the spirit world was more important.

"I think I'd like to talk to my uncle Jasper," Cook decided. "He was so much fun. He knew stories and jokes — oh, he made us all laugh. I'll never forget him."

Mr. Not So Much pricked up his ears. He, too, once had an uncle he would never forget. His uncle had not been full of jokes and stories, though. He was nothing like Cook's uncle. His name had been Phineas Skoff, and he had been a tall, frown-faced man with a bony chin and bony fingers. Mr. Not So Much bore a remarkable resemblance to him.

Uncle Phineas had been very rich. Everything he touched turned to money. He had always promised Mr. Not So Much he would tell him his secret of gaining riches.

But he had died and taken the secret with him into the spirit world beyond.

Mr. Not So Much sat down in his chair again, quietly. He was not so eager to leave now. Perhaps if Miss Lavender really could speak to the spirit world, this might be his chance to contact Uncle Phineas.

No one paid any attention to Mr. Not So Much. "Can we really have a séance?" Cook was saying. And then the parlor table was cleared and Miss Lavender said, "Draw up your chairs. Draw up your chairs around the table."

Tatty and Phoebe scrambled up from the floor to get chairs.

Miss Plum was doubtful that people who had "gone on" came back for chats, but she could see that both Cook and Miss Lavender were eager to try.

Little Ann was settled in a rocking chair and pushed up to the table. Cook arranged her hair a bit in case Uncle Jasper could see her as she spoke.

They were ready to begin.

Calling Uncle Jasper

"We must all join hands," Miss Lavender said.

She put her own hands on the table and took hold of Tatty's on one side and Miss Plum's on the other.

Miss Plum also took Little Ann's hand,
Little Ann took Cook's hand,
Cook took Phoebe's hand,
Phoebe took Tatty's hand,
and the circle was complete.

"Perhaps a little less light," Miss Lavender said.

Phoebe darted away from the table and turned off the parlor lamp. Miss Plum drew the drapes. Only the glowing fire lit the dim room.

Everyone had forgotten Mr. Not So Much in his chair in the corner. He was now almost lost in shadow; he was also lost in thought. If Miss Lavender really could speak to people who had gone beyond, he intended to ask for a turn at the table and talk to Uncle Phineas, and learn at last the secret of making money.

Phoebe slipped back into place and grasped hands again. Cook's hand was plump and warm, trembling a little with expectation. Tatty's hand was sticky from a jam sandwich she had recently eaten.

Miss Plum came from the windows and took her place again.

"First I must go into my trance," Miss Lavender explained. "I've seen it done, so I believe I know how."

Miss Plum was too polite to mention that Miss Lavender had also seen hypnotism done, and had failed at that.

Miss Lavender closed her eyes. She tilted her head back slightly and began to call upon the spirit world. "Oh, hear me, spirits . . . oh, hear me, spirits."

Everyone at the table waited silently.

"Are you there, spirits?"

Little Ann looked up into the air to see what Miss Lavender was looking at. She saw only firelight shadows and the parlor ceiling.

"Are you there, spirits? Is Cook's Uncle Jasper there?"

No one dared breathe.

"Uncle Jasper . . . if you are there, speak to your dear niece — our dear Cook."

Tatty gave Phoebe's hand a secret squeeze. Phoebe gave Tatty a nudge under the table with her foot. Little Ann looked up at the ceiling until her neck hurt.

The fire sputtered in the fireplace, burning low. It needed a new log, but no one moved from the séance table to put one on. Shadows lengthened along the wall, darkening in the corners. Mr. Not So Much, lost in the gloom, began to feel doubtful. No spirits seemed to be answering Miss Lavender's urgent calls.

"Uncle Jasper . . . if you are there, speak

to your niece . . . she is waiting . . . she loves you so much. . . ."

Waiting for Uncle Jasper was like waiting for The Great Rudolpho. It came to nothing. Only the echo of silence followed Miss Lavender's calls for the spirits to speak. Little Ann and Tatty began to wriggle. Phoebe nudged Tatty with her foot again. And then worst of all, Tatty began to giggle.

"I think we must stop," Miss Plum said. "It's time for the girls to wash up for dinner."

Cook gave a long sigh. "I don't think Uncle Jasper is going to speak to me," she said.

Mr. Not So Much was disappointed, too — and irritated. He had wasted precious time in this foolishness. He should have left long ago. He should be home by now. Instead he had stayed on and wasted all his time. Uncle Phineas would never speak to him from the spirit world. He would never know the secret of great riches.

Mr. Not So Much was so upset, he hardly noticed the movements in the parlor. Cook drew open the curtains. Phoebe turned on the parlor lamp. Miss Plum stoked up the fire. And Tatty pushed the chairs back into their right places.

"I think we need another log," Miss Plum said from the fireside.

"Here, Tatty, let me help you with that chair," Cook said.

Only Miss Lavender remained at her place at the séance table. Her head was still slightly back. Now that the fire was burning more brightly and the lamp turned on, everyone could see that her eyes were still closed.

"Oh, spirits, speak to us . . . speak to us . . ." Miss Lavender called out in a clear voice. It was a voice sure to reach the spirit world, if the spirit world was listening.

Miss Plum came toward the séance table, the fire poker still in her hand. She peered at Miss Lavender uncertainly. "I do believe

Miss Lavender is still in her trance," she said.

Tatty, Phoebe, and Little Ann came running to see.

Cook, too, came toward the table.

"Well, the séance has not been entirely unsuccessful," Miss Plum said slowly. "Whether or not the spirits answered, Miss Lavender is definitely in a trance."

Commotion in the Parlor

At first Miss Plum was calm. She patted Miss Lavender's hands to see if that would snap her out of the trance. "Wake up, Miss Lavender. The séance is over." Miss Plum shook Miss Lavender gently.

Then a little more firmly.

And then even more firmly.

Miss Lavender's eyes didn't open. Her head remained slightly tilted back in her trance position. "Uncle Jasper . . . are you there . . . ?" she called.

"Perhaps a damp cloth for her forehead." Cook looked anxious.

"Just the thing." Miss Plum sent Phoebe scurrying for a damp cloth. Tatty and Little Ann ran along with Phoebe, though it didn't take three girls to carry one damp cloth.

Mr. Not So Much remained silent in his

corner, sunk in his own bleak thoughts of Uncle Phineas and his great wealth. He was vaguely aware of the girls running past him, but he paid little attention. "Not so much running," he mumbled without stirring in his chair.

"Miss Lavender, the séance is over." Miss Plum gave Miss Lavender a few more firm shakes.

Cook got very upset. "If I hadn't wanted to talk to my uncle Jasper, this never would have happened," she said.

When Phoebe, Tatty, and Little Ann raced back with the cool damp cloth, Mr. Not So Much became more aware of the activity around him. It was hard not to take notice. Behind Phoebe, Tatty, and Little Ann came:

Kate,
Elsie May,
Mary,
Nonnie,
six other girls,
and a black kitten with four white paws.

The girls bumped into each other to get close around the table.

"There," said Miss Plum, laying the cloth gently on Miss Lavender's brow. "Doesn't that feel good, Miss Lavender? Wake up now, the séance is over."

The girls crowded even closer.

"Oh, spirits . . . speak to us . . . speak to us."

The damp cloth was not working.

"She's forgotten how to come out of a trance," Miss Plum said. She reached out to pat Miss Lavender's hand and shake her. But Miss Lavender caught hold of Miss Plum and held her tight. There stood Miss Plum, the fire poker still in one hand, Miss Lavender gripping her other hand.

Miss Plum began to feel desperate.

Cook ran to the kitchen and came back with a glass of cold water. "This might wake her if we toss it in her face," Cook said a little uncertainly.

"That seems unkind," Miss Plum said.

A loud discussion followed. Should they

throw cold water at Miss Lavender? Or shouldn't they? The parlor was so noisy that Mr. Not So Much finally became fully aware of the commotion around him.

He turned in his chair and squarely faced the table. Girls were bobbing about like corks at sea. Cook and Miss Plum were talking at once, with rising voices. The kitten, unattended, clawed its way up a curtain toward the ceiling of the room. Several girls had climbed up on chairs and tables to see better, and Little Ann fell off a chair arm and began to cry.

It was more than Mr. Not So Much could bear.

"NOT SO MUCH FOOLISHNESS!" he roared, springing from his chair with a creak of bones and fire in his eyes.

Miss Lavender was jolted out of her trance as though she had been struck a blow.

No trance in the world could have survived that angry bellow.

A Surprise

After that, Miss Lavender was cured of wanting to talk to those who had "gone on" to the spirit world. She was cured of wanting to hypnotize anyone. She seemed to be cured of wanting to do magic.

When The Good Day girls got home from school in the afternoons, Miss Lavender was mending, or planning grocery lists with Cook, or writing letters to friends, and other nice things like that. She was not trying to do magic. Everyone thought she had forgotten all about it.

And then one day, when it was nearly winter, Miss Lavender came into the parlor carrying a large brown paper bag. Miss Plum noticed that she looked very pleased with herself. "What are you up to, Miss Lavender?" she asked.

"It's a surprise," Miss Lavender said.

She sat down on the sofa and put the paper bag on the floor beside her.

Just at that moment, Phoebe and Kate came by the parlor door, pretending to be explorers at the North Pole, tracking polar bears in the snow. When they found the polar bears, they would run for their lives so the polar bears wouldn't eat them.

Before this dash for their lives could begin, Miss Lavender called to them to come into the parlor. "I have a surprise to show all of you," she said. "I want you to find the other girls and bring them here. It's a very exciting surprise."

"Cook may come, too," Miss Lavender called after Kate and Phoebe as they raced away.

Twenty-six girls are not rounded up in a moment.

Kate had to put on a jacket and run outside to find the girls who were playing in the park.

Phoebe pounded upstairs and knocked on bedroom doors.

Little Ann had taken off her shoes and stockings to wade in a bathtub. It took time to dry her off.

Elsie May had just washed her hair and had to come with her head in a towel. This made her mad because she was very vain. But she didn't want to miss anything.

Tatty and Nonnie were making scrapbook paste with flour and water. It hadn't turned out well. Their fingers and dresses were splotched with sticky white paste. They cleaned up as best they could and ran downstairs to the parlor.

Agnes was drawing a map of Africa for her geography class.

Mary was writing a poem.

Winter is coming
Snowflakes will fly
Down on my head
Out of the sky

"Come on, come on," Phoebe urged everyone. "Miss Lavender has a surprise."

Kate came back from the park, breathless and red-cheeked. She was followed by seven girls she had found playing tag.

Then Cook was called from the kitchen so she could be in on the surprise, too. She came wiping her hands on her apron, smelling a bit of cinnamon and other spices.

Miss Lavender was still sitting on the sofa, the large brown paper bag beside her.

The girls gathered around curiously. They sat on chairs and chair arms, on the floor, three on the piano bench, two on a stool by the fire. A cheery fire burned in the grate and the mantel clock was near to striking for five o'clock. Outside, full darkness had come.

When everyone was settled, Miss Lavender said, "I would like to give a demonstration."

Miss Plum and Cook felt rather nervous hearing this. They didn't want Miss Lavender to go into another trance.

"A demonstration of the spirit world?" Cook asked cautiously.

"No, indeed." Miss Lavender shook her head mysteriously.

"Hypnotism?" Miss Plum asked, also cautiously.

"Not hypnotism." Miss Lavender shook her head again.

"Then — what?"

Miss Lavender smiled a smile of great satisfaction. "Magic," she said.

"*Magic! Magic!*" All the girls were thrilled.

"Magic?" Miss Plum was amazed. "You have finally learned magic, Miss Lavender?"

"Well" — Miss Lavender wanted to make herself clear — "I have learned *one* magic thing, and I would like to show it to you."

"My," said Cook, "isn't this exciting?"

Then Miss Lavender lifted the brown paper bag onto her lap. As everyone watched, she took out a wand.

It was a wand she had made herself with silver paper wrapped around a stick. It was very beautiful, very magical. Every girl instantly wanted one just like it.

Phoebe and Kate forgot the North Pole polar bears (though they might come back after supper and chase them up and down the stairs until bedtime, and roar terrible roars).

Tatty forgot all the arithmetic answers she had learned that day at school. She stood close by the sofa and waited to see what would happen next.

Miss Lavender took the tall black magician's hat she had bought from The Great Rudolpho out of the paper bag.

"You kept it," Tatty said. She was the closest to Miss Lavender and she reached out to touch the silky side of the wonderful hat.

"Yes, I kept it," Miss Lavender said. She smiled around at her large audience.

"Let us all be quiet now," Miss Plum told the girls. "I think Miss Lavender is going to do something magic for us — after all."

What else could it be but magic, with a wand and magician's hat!

There was a hush in the parlor. Only the tick of the mantel clock could be heard. (Miss Plum had remembered to wind it only that morning.)

In the midst of this intense quiet, Miss Lavender waved her silvery wand across the black hat. Then she reached deep down into the hat and pulled out a rabbit.

It was a plump, fluffy white rabbit. Its nose was pink and quivering. It nestled in her hands and blinked its ruby-red eyes.

For a long moment, the parlor was silent. And then a shout of voices began.

"You did it!"

"You learned magic!"

"A rabbit in a hat!"

Everyone was talking at once.

It was a wonderful moment of triumph for Miss Lavender. She smiled at everyone — and then, without a word, she put the rabbit back into the hat.

The girls sighed in disappointment.

"I wanted to pet it," Little Ann said, with a finger in her mouth.

"Me, too."

"Me, too."

All the girls had wanted to pet the fluffy white rabbit with the trembly pink nose.

Tatty, closest of all, leaned forward and looked into the hat. Other girls crowded around, trying to look into the hat. Miss Lavender held it out for them to see.

The hat was quite empty.

Miss Lavender held the hat upside down and gave it a good shake. No rabbit tumbled out.

"Where did it go?" Phoebe asked. They stared at Miss Lavender with open mouths and wide eyes.

Miss Lavender only smiled mysteriously. "That's the magic part," she said. "True magic. I told The Great Rudolpho that true magic shouldn't need real rabbits. And it doesn't."

"But how — ?"

"But how — ?"

The girls clamored around Miss Lavender, begging to know the secret of this

true magic. Cook was as wide-eyed as the girls.

Miss Lavender only smiled a mysterious smile. "I was sure I could do it," she said. "I kept practicing."

"And it was a good thing you kept the hat," Cook added.

"Yes," Miss Lavender agreed. "I thought the hat might come in handy some day, and it did."

Then she put the black hat and the wand back into the brown paper bag.

She was happy that she could at last do something magic.

How she did it was her own secret.

No one else ever knew.